curious about

# LEGO

BY RACHEL GRACK

# What are you

# curious about?

CHAPTER THREE

## 3

## Bet You Didn't Know...

PAGE

## 18

Curious About is published by Amicus
P.O. Box 227
Mankato, MN 56002
www.amicuspublishing.us

Editor: Alissa Thielges
Series and Book Designer: Kathleen Petelinsek
Cover Designer: Lori Bye
Photo researcher: Omay Ayres

Library of Congress Cataloging-in-Publication Data
Names: Koestler-Grack, Rachel A., 1973– author.
Title: Curious about LEGO / by Rachel Grack.
Description: Mankato, MN: Amicus, [2024] | Series: Curious about favorite brands | Includes bibliographical references and index. | Audience: Ages 5–9 | Audience: Grades 2–3 | Summary: "Nine kid-friendly questions give elementary readers an inside look at LEGO to spark their curiosity about the brand's history and products. A Stay Curious! feature models research skills while simple infographics support visual literacy" — Provided by publisher.
Identifiers: LCCN 2022032139 (print) | LCCN 2022032140 (ebook) | ISBN 9781645493273 (library binding) | ISBN 9781681528519 (paperback) | ISBN 9781645494157 (ebook)
Subjects: LCSH: LEGO toys—Juvenile literature. | LEGO koncernen (Denmark)—History—Juvenile literature.
Classification: LCC TS2301.T7 K64 2024 (print) | LCC TS2301. T7 (ebook) | DDC 688.7/25—dc23/eng/20220901
LC record available at https://lccn.loc.gov/2022032139
LC ebook record available at https://lccn.loc.gov/2022032140

Photos © Alamy/PictureLux/The Hollywood Archive 21, Reuters 13, Sam Stephenson 5, Wojciech Strózyk 18–19; Dreamstime/Aguina 16 (California), Chengusf 16 (Florida), Chengusf 7 (t), FabioConcetta 7 (b), Renata Tyburczy 16 (New York), Senatorjoanna 17 (Denmark); iStock/juniorbeep, cover; The LEGO Group 9; Shutterstock/AlesiaKan 10–11, 14–15, anastas_styles 16 (UK), askarim 12, Ekaterina_Minaeva 6 (t), 20, Irina Rogova 17 (Germany), Jsita 17 (Japan), Martial Red 22, 23, ovbelov 17 (UAE), Radu Bercan 6 (b), Vivi Ramadhani 17 (Malaysia); Wikimedia Commons 4, 5

Printed in China

# Where did LEGO come from?

PLAY WELL

**Ole Kirk Kristiansen**

Kiddicraft first had the idea. The company made plastic bricks that could stack together. Ole Kirk Kristiansen liked the idea. He started LEGO in Denmark in 1936. LEGO is named after the Danish words *leg go*dt. It means "play well." In 1949, he began selling the toy bricks. These were the first LEGO pieces!

LEGO bricks were inspired by other building bricks.

LEGO minifigures

# Does LEGO sell only bricks?

You can buy much more than bricks in this LEGO store in Romania.

Bine ați venit!

You can stay at this hotel in the LEGOLAND in Florida.

Not anymore. Those tiny bricks built the largest toy company in the world! The **brand** also sells books, puzzles, and board games. Its minifigures are characters in movies and video games. LEGO even has ten **amusement parks**. Bricks are still an all-time favorite. LEGO believes in learning through play.

## DID YOU KNOW?

LEGO bricks haven't changed since 1958. Missing a piece? See if your friends have one you can borrow.

# What was the first LEGO set?

Until 1955, kids used only their imaginations for building. Then LEGO made sets with instructions for building. The first LEGO set was a one-car garage. Other sets soon followed. People started collecting them to build a whole LEGO town. Sets today can have hundreds of pieces. They take hours to put together.

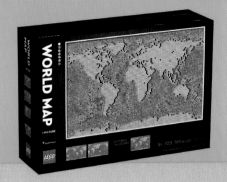

**WORLD MAP**
**11,695 PIECES**

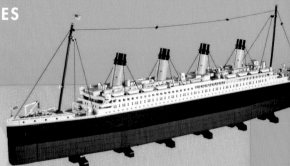

**TITANIC**
**9,090 PIECES**

**COLOSSEUM**
**9,036 PIECES**

*STAR WARS*
**MILLENNIUM FALCON**
**7,541 PIECES**

*HARRY POTTER*
**HOGWARTS CASTLE**
**6,020 PIECES**

You can build cat or dog robots.

# Can I build LEGO sets that move?

Sure! Many LEGO sets come with wheels, hinges, and propellers. Build your own moving parts with gears and axles. Robot sets even move on their own! You can **program** the robots to do lots of cool things. Give commands from your tablet or cell phone. Maybe you can program one to clean your room.

# CHAPTER TWO

# What is it like to work at LEGO?

LEGO headquarters in Billund, Denmark

LEGO **designers** play hard all day! They work in Denmark. First, they draw out their ideas. Next, they hit the LEGO library. It holds every LEGO piece ever made. They collect a pile of bricks and start building. It takes time and teamwork to complete each set. Sounds like fun!

Nathan Sawaya, a LEGO artist, poses beside his creation "Blue Guy Sitting."

# How can I show off my building skills?

**Boys and girls build and code robots.**

Enter a LEGO contest! Some schools have FIRST LEGO League teams. It is a great way to practice. Students of the same ages **compete** against each other. Have you ever watched the TV show *LEGO Masters*? Players face off to prove who is the best brick builder. Maybe you could be next!

**DID YOU KNOW?**
Some people build LEGO models for a living. They are called Master Model Builders.

# What is LEGOLAND?

United Kingdom

California

New York

Florida

Picture a park built with LEGOs! All the rides and **attractions** look like LEGO sets. Families can even take classes to learn brick building tricks. Every park has its own Miniland. These show LEGO models of popular places from each city. There are parks all around the world.

Denmark

Germany

Japan

United
Arab
Emirates

Malaysia

# CHAPTER THREE

# What is the biggest LEGO model ever made?

The X-Wing was
built in Denmark and
moved to California.

For now, it's a *Star Wars* X-Wing. It took 17,000 hours and 32 people to build. It has more than 5 million bricks! The spaceship is a life-size model. It was displayed at LEGOLAND in California. The X-Wing broke the record of Herobot 9000. This robot guards the LEGO store at the Mall of America in Minnesota. It stands 34 feet (10 meters) tall.

# Do LEGO movies use real bricks?

Yes. Some scenes are built by hand. Others use **digital** bricks. They are put together with computers. Everything on screen is made of bricks. That includes smoke, water, fire, and explosions. It looks just like a real LEGO set. Some pieces even show fingerprints from play. LEGO keeps its promise to make learning fun.

**DID YOU KNOW?**
The *LEGO Movie* used more than 15 million bricks.

*The LEGO Movie*
was a box office hit!

## ASK MORE QUESTIONS

**How do I learn how to free build with LEGOs?**

**Can I make a LEGO movie?**

**Try a BIG QUESTION: What skills do Master Model Builders need?**

## SEARCH FOR ANSWERS

**Search the library catalog or the Internet.**
A librarian, teacher, or parent can help you.

**Using Keywords**
Find the looking glass.

🔍

**Keywords are the most important words in your question.**

?

**If you want to know:**

- what to free build, type: LEGO BUILD IDEAS
- how to make a movie, type: MAKE A LEGO MOVIE

# FIND GOOD SOURCES

## Are the sources reliable?

Some sources are better than others. An adult can help you. Here are some good, safe sources.

## Books

**LEGO**
by Martha London, 2020.

**LEGO Bricks**
by Chris Bowman, 2022.

## Internet Sites

**LEGO for Kids**
*https://www.lego.com/en-us/kids*
LEGO for Kids is an interactive website with games, videos, and LEGO news.

**TED-ed: How fan films shaped The LEGO Movie**
*https://ed.ted.com/best_of_web/U1towgtz*
TED-ed is a non-profit educational site with videos on many topics.

Every effort has been made to ensure that these websites are appropriate for children. However, because of the nature of the Internet, it is impossible to guarantee that these sites will remain active indefinitely or that their contents will not be altered.

# SHARE AND TAKE ACTION

**Download Studio BrickLink for free.**
Use it to create LEGO models using digital bricks.

**Organize a class LEGO building contest.**
Come up with a theme. Let everyone vote for their favorite design.

**Become a LEGO designer!**
Do you have a great idea for a LEGO kit? Share it on the "LEGO Ideas" page. If your idea gets 10,000 likes, it might become the next LEGO set in stores!
*https://ideas.lego.com/projects/create*

# GLOSSARY

**amusement park** A large outdoor park with rides, activities, and restaurants.

**attraction** A building, statue, fun activity, or other interesting thing that draws people's attention.

**brand** A group of products made or owned by the same company.

**compete** To try to outdo other people in order to win something.

**designer** Someone who works ideas into a new product.

**digital** Having to do with computers or electronics.

**program** To give a computer a set of instructions to perform a particular action.

# INDEX

## About the Author

Rachel Grack has been editing and writing children's books since 1999. She lives on a small ranch in southern Arizona. As a lover of stories, Disney is close to her heart. She also enjoys watching her grandchildren play Pokémon games on her Nintendo 64 console.